NATURE SMARTS
WORKBOOK
AGES 7–9

- - - - - - - - - - - - - - - - - - - -

**From the
Environmental
Educators of**
 **Mass Audubon**

Storey Publishing

The mission of Storey Publishing is to serve our customers by publishing practical information that encourages personal independence in harmony with the environment.

Edited by Deanna F. Cook, Hannah Fries, and
    Lisa H. Hiley
Art direction and book design by Alethea Morrison
Text production by Jennifer Jepson Smith
Illustrations by © Jada Fitch

Storey books are available at special discounts when purchased in bulk for premiums and sales promotions as well as for fund-raising or educational use. Special editions or book excerpts can also be created to specification. For details, please call 800-827-8673, or send an email to sales@storey.com.

Storey Publishing
210 MASS MoCA Way
North Adams, MA 01247
storey.com

Printed in the United States by Lakeside Book Company
10 9 8 7 6 5 4 3 2 1

MADE in the USA

Library of Congress Cataloging-in-Publication Data on file

CONTENTS

Nature Is Everywhere

To find nature near you, just step outside and start exploring! Look for a spider building a web or some ants carrying food along the sidewalk. Feel the wind blowing past your face. Listen for birds singing or leaves rustling. Take a deep breath to smell some flowers. You can learn about nature wherever you are!

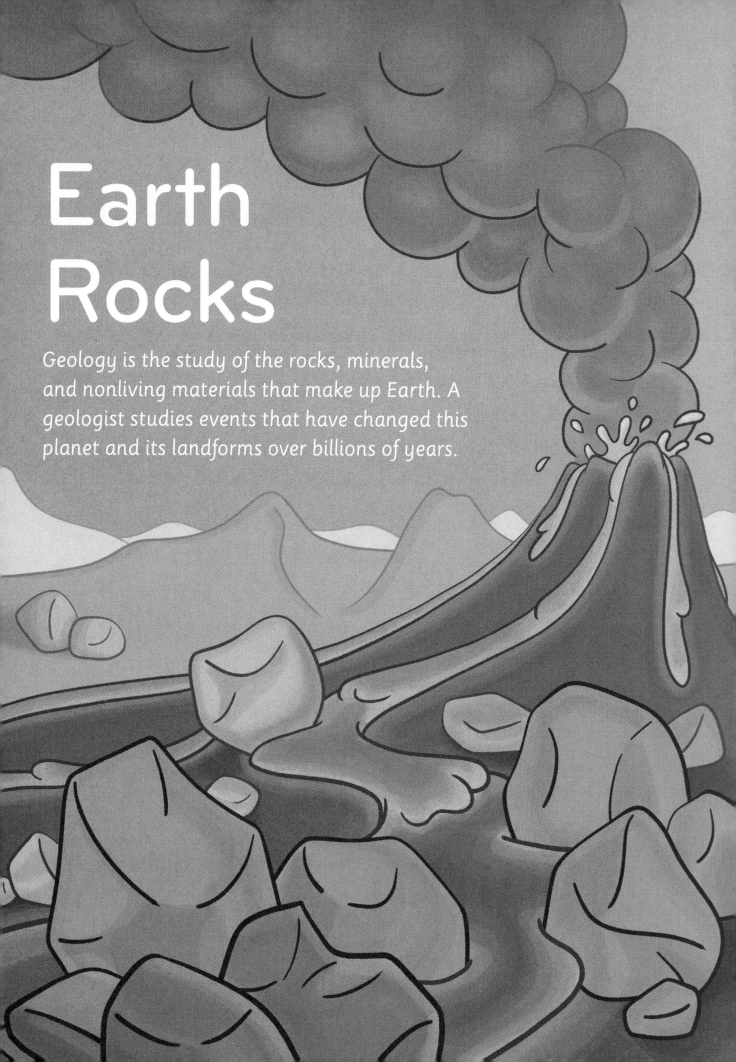

Earth Rocks

Geology is the study of the rocks, minerals, and nonliving materials that make up Earth. A geologist studies events that have changed this planet and its landforms over billions of years.

Mapping the Land

Maps give us a big picture of where things are. We can use a map to show the many landforms that give shape to our marvelous planet Earth.

➤ Fill in all the blank labels on this map with the name of the landforms, using the key below.

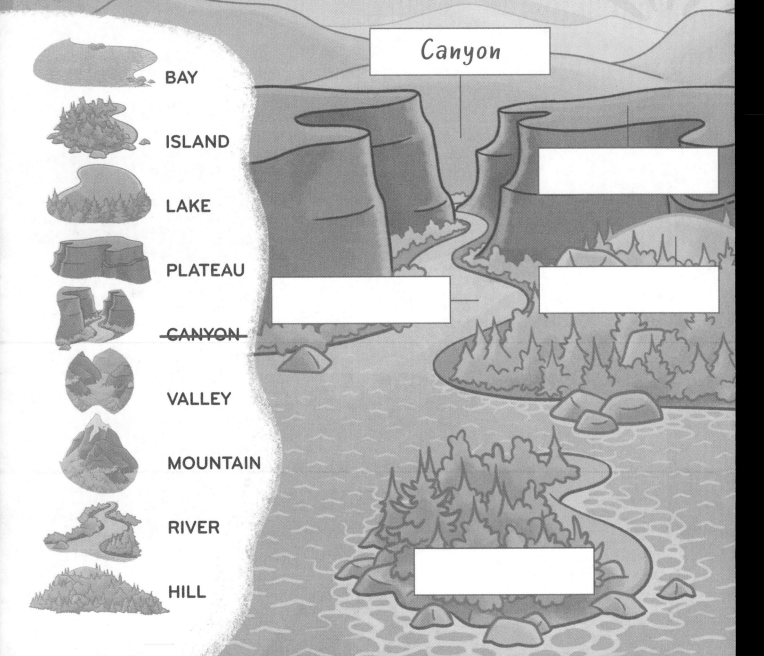

BAY

ISLAND

LAKE

PLATEAU

~~CANYON~~

VALLEY

MOUNTAIN

RIVER

HILL

Canyon

FUN FACT
Scientists estimate that planet Earth is about 4.5 BILLION years old. The oldest rocks found so far are in Canada. They are about 4.3 billion years old.

Answer key on page 93

Eroding Away

Both weathering and erosion are constantly changing the earth's surface. WEATHERING is how rocks and minerals are broken down into small pieces. EROSION is when these small pieces of rock and soil are carried from one place to another by wind, water, or other natural forces.

➤ Look at the picture at left and then compare it to the picture below. Draw a circle around the changes that have occurred in the picture on this page as a result of weathering and erosion.

FUN FACT
The Grand Canyon was created by erosion. The Colorado River carved it out over millions and millions of years.

Answer key on page 93

Rock Explorer

One way that geologists sort rocks is by how they are formed.

➤ Match the words in orange below with the pictures. Fill in the blanks to complete the name of each type of rock.

IGNEOUS rocks are formed when hot molten materials cool and turn solid. Igneous rocks can form underground, beneath the Earth's surface, or aboveground from lava. GRANITE and OBSIDIAN are examples of igneous rocks.

SEDIMENTARY rocks are formed when many layers of sand, mud, and small rock build up and are squished together under pressure. SANDSTONE and CONGLOMERATE are examples of sedimentary rocks.

METAMORPHIC rocks are transformed from one type of rock to a different type of rock when exposed to high heat and pressure. GNEISS (pronounced "nice") and QUARTZITE are examples of metamorphic rocks.

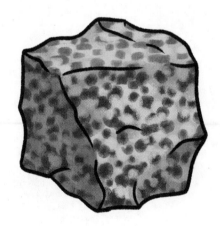

G_ _ _ _ _ _

G_ _ _ _ _ _ _ _ _

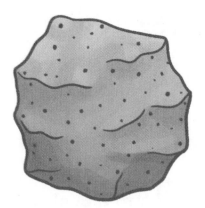

S_ _ _ _ _ _ _ _ _ _ _ _ _

Q_ _ _ _ _ _ _ _ _ _ _

O_ _ _ _ _ _ _ _ _

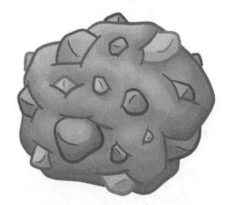

C_ _ _ _ _ _ _ _ _ _ _ _ _

The Rock Cycle

Over long periods of time, rocks can change from one type of rock into another.

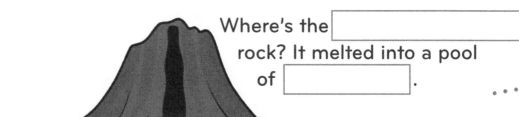

Where's the [＿＿＿＿＿＿] rock? It melted into a pool of [＿＿＿＿＿＿].

Deep in the earth under extreme heat and pressure, [＿＿＿＿＿＿] rock turns into **METAMORPHIC** rock.

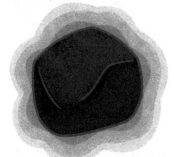

Over a long time, layers of [＿＿＿＿＿＿] build up and get squished under lots of other layers. Now it is a **SEDIMENTARY** rock.

The pieces get smaller and smaller. Finally, the river deposits them as **SEDIMENT**.

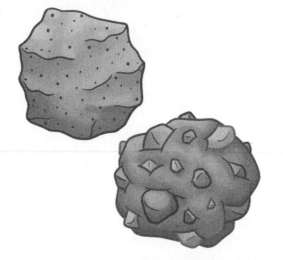

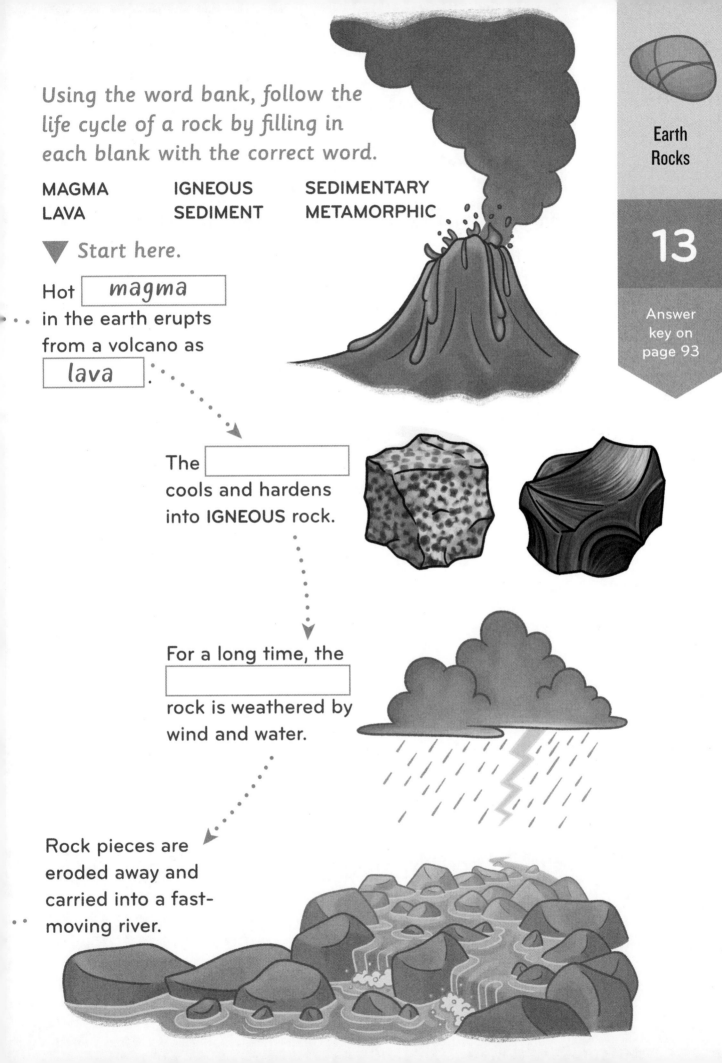

Using the word bank, follow the life cycle of a rock by filling in each blank with the correct word.

MAGMA   IGNEOUS   SEDIMENTARY
LAVA   SEDIMENT   METAMORPHIC

▼ Start here.

Hot *magma* in the earth erupts from a volcano as *lava* .

The _____ cools and hardens into **IGNEOUS** rock.

For a long time, the _____ rock is weathered by wind and water.

Rock pieces are eroded away and carried into a fast-moving river.

Write Your Own Rock Story

Think about all the processes (weathering, erosion, heat, pressure) that change rocks from one type of rock to another. Write a short story about a small rock and the exciting adventures it went through becoming different kinds of rocks. How does your rock feel about going through all these big changes?

Rock Out: Word Search

➤ The 14 words listed below are hidden in the grid. Draw a circle around each one.

```
S K U P Y W P Z M H K F L N O
B G K E R O S I O N P P D D N
F T Q B O S R J U P L U R H A
J V B H C V D J N A E R O T C
L G E O L O G Y T L N V C Q L
J A Y F H L Z E A M O N K E O
T A M G A M A V I X E D R A V
M A K I B U A W N I D U X H V
E K C Z C I H P R O M A T E M
V S U O E N G I E Y X Z H F K
T J T M Z G R E Y A D A X P I
E M L L D Y G V L K N O B O J
H B S E D I M E N T A R Y R O
Q L T G V V M I N E R A L R X
P R E S S U R E X L A L T T I
```

LAVA   EROSION   PLATEAU

MAGMA   PRESSURE   GEOLOGY

IGNEOUS   HEAT   MINERAL

SEDIMENTARY   VOLCANO   ROCK

METAMORPHIC   MOUNTAIN

Rock Collector

You can study geology just by walking out your front door! Go out for a walk and collect as many different types of rocks as you can find. Can you find rocks that match the descriptions below?

GRAY	WHITE

REDDISH BROWN	SHINY

FUN FACT
ROCK HOUND is a fun name given to people who collect rocks, minerals, gems, and fossils as a hobby. You can look up rockhounding maps online for ideas of where to look for gems, fossils, and more near you!

➤ Sort your rocks by placing them inside the boxes on these pages.

SPARKLY	STRIPED

ROUGH	SMOOTH

What are some other ways to sort them?

Frozen in Time

Fossils are evidence of plants and animals that lived millions of years ago (that's a long time!). There are fossils of leaves, roots, bones, shells, animal tracks, eggs, and even dinosaur scat (poop)!

Fossils have been found all over the world. Scientists study them to learn about the plants or animals that lived in a place long ago.

Many fossils were formed when an organism (a living being) died, was covered by sediment, and became part of the sedimentary rock. Sometimes an organism became trapped in tree resin that hardened into amber.

FUN FACT
Fossilized animal droppings are called **COPROLITES**.

➤ Draw a line from each organism on the left to the fossil that matches it on the right.

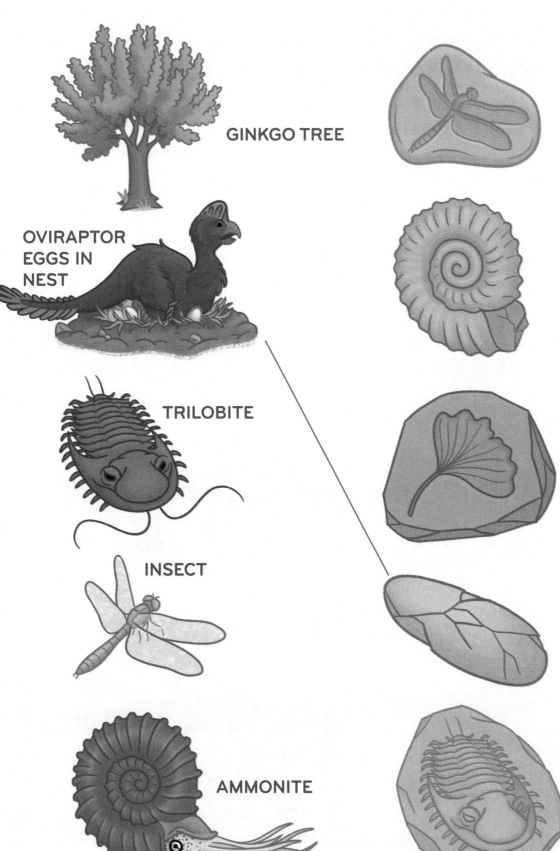

GINKGO TREE

OVIRAPTOR EGGS IN NEST

TRILOBITE

INSECT

AMMONITE

Tracks Tell a Tale

Fossilized bones aren't the only evidence of dinosaurs. Many ancient creatures also left behind footprints that can tell us a lot about how big they were and how they moved. A series of tracks is called a **TRACKWAY**.

CHIROTHERIUM (KY-roh-THEE-ree-um) dinosaurs had five toes on each foot. The hind feet were larger than the front ones.

SAUROPODS (SAW-roh-pods) needed big, round feet to support their large size and long necks.

THEROPOD (THEH-roh-pod) dinosaurs walked on strong hind legs. They had three toes with claws on each foot.

➤ Use this space to draw a dinosaur of your
   own. What kind of footprints would it leave?

Make Your Own Fossil

Looking for actual fossils is amazing, but if you can't head out on an expedition, you can have fun making models of fossils at home with some items you might already have in your kitchen.

HERE IS WHAT YOU WILL NEED.

1 cup used coffee grounds

1 cup all-purpose flour

½ cup salt

½ cup cold coffee or water

Wax paper

Empty glass or can

Small objects to create the fossil impressions (such as toy dinosaurs, seashells, starfish)

Directions for making your own fossil.

1 Mix the coffee grounds, flour, and salt together in a bowl. Slowly add the coffee or water a little at a time and mix with the dry ingredients until the mixture forms a dough. (The coffee grounds and coffee aren't essential, but they will make your fossils look like you just discovered them in the dirt!)

2 Scoop the dough out onto a sheet of wax paper. Knead for 3 to 4 minutes, until the dough holds its shape and becomes less sticky.

3 Pat the dough out into a rectangular shape about ½ inch thick. Use the glass or can to cut circles out of the dough.

4 Press the small objects firmly into the dough to create imprints. Remove the objects from the dough.

5 With the assistance of an adult, bake the dough fossils at 200°F (93°C) for 45 minutes or until hard. Larger or thicker fossils may take longer to completely harden.

BE A NATURE HERO

Prevent Soil Erosion!

Soil erosion happens when the top layer of soil washes away. Erosion can happen in fields and farmlands, along driveways, and even in parks and backyards. Many plants not only keep soil in place but also provide habitat for wildlife.

Adding a few plants to a bare patch of ground is an easy way to conserve and protect soil in your neighborhood. Try it!

1. Head outside for a walk and look for bare patches of dirt.

2. Notice what kinds of plants are nearby. Can you find some seeds from those plants? You can collect them to plant in a new place.

3. If not, you can buy grass or wildflower seeds at a local store or nursery.

4. Following the directions on the packet, plant the seeds in bare patches and take care of them until they start to grow.

CONEFLOWER

YARROW

PHLOX

Our Planet Earth

Earth is our home planet. It is the third planet from the sun. This is our place in space.

Earth is currently the only planet known to have life. Our planet has the oxygen we need to breathe and the water we need to drink. Water covers almost three-fourths of Earth's surface or about 71 percent. Living things on Earth depend on our planet's natural systems and cycles.

Planet Puzzle

The sun is the center of our solar system. The sun is a star made of hot gases that provide heat and light. It is the closest star to our home planet, Earth, but the sun is 100 times bigger than Earth. All of the planets in our solar system revolve around the sun.

EARTH is the only planet we have found with life on it. It is third from the sun.

JUPITER is the largest planet, twice the size of all the other planets combined.

MERCURY is closest to the sun. It rotates around the sun every 88 Earth days.

VENUS is the hottest of the planets and spins clockwise on its axis, which is the opposite direction of most planets.

MARS is often called the "red planet" and is currently home to four robots sent by NASA (the official space agency of the United States). It is between Earth and Jupiter.

SATURN has rings of ice and rock around it.

URANUS also has rings but spins on its side. It is between Saturn and Neptune.

NEPTUNE is farthest from the sun, nearly 3 billion miles. This distance makes it both very dark and cold.

➤ Using what you learned about the planets on page 26, can you correctly label the planets in order from the closest to the sun to the farthest away?

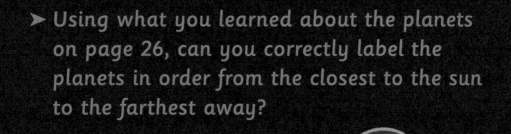

Sun

Star Maps

Humans all over the world have looked up in the sky and have seen pictures in the stars. Many people say the pictures tell stories. These star pictures are called **CONSTELLATIONS**. A constellation might take the shape of an animal, a person, or an object such as a big spoon (or "dipper").

LEO

EXPLORE OUTSIDE!

As the earth turns throughout the year, the stars appear to change position in the sky.

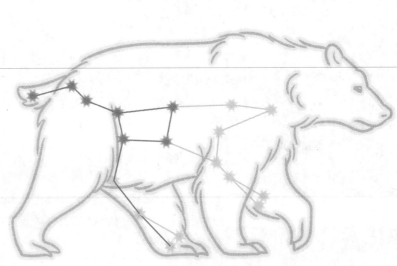

GREAT BEAR
(Big Dipper)

➤ What do you see in the sky? Draw your own picture using the stars in these constellations. (To see the traditional shapes, turn to the answer key.)

ORION

DRACO

PEGASUS

Welcome to the Water Cycle

Water comes and goes but never completely disappears. We call this the **WATER CYCLE**.

➤ *Fill in the blanks to complete the words of the water cycle. Look at the picture on the left for clues.*

The energy from the sun heats up the water on Earth, from puddles to ponds and streams to seas. The heated water molecules float into the air as water vapor, which is a gas. This is called

E __ __ __ __ __ __ __ __ __ __ __.

Water vapor travels on the wind, high into the sky. As the molecules cool, they collect together to form clouds. This is called

C __ __ __ __ __ __ __ __ __ __ __ __ __.

The water molecules cling together in droplets. When the droplets become heavy enough, they form

P __ __ __ __ __ __ __ __ __ __ __ __ __

and fall to the ground as rain, hail, sleet, or snow.

Rain or melting snow flows into

B __ __ __ __ __ OF W __ __ __ __

from puddles to oceans. A puddle will evaporate quickly in the sun. The ocean has so much water, it never completely evaporates.

Measuring Precipitation

Precipitation (when water falls to the ground as rain or snow) is a big part of the water cycle. It is how we get most of the fresh water on the planet. Some parts of the world experience much more precipitation than others. The same parts of one landmass might experience more precipitation in one season and less in another.

This map uses colors to show how much precipitation falls in different parts of the United States in one year.

➤ Look at the map and color key. Draw a circle around the state that has the least amount of precipitation.

<10 inches
11–19 inches
20–29 inches
30–39 inches
40–49 inches
50+ inches

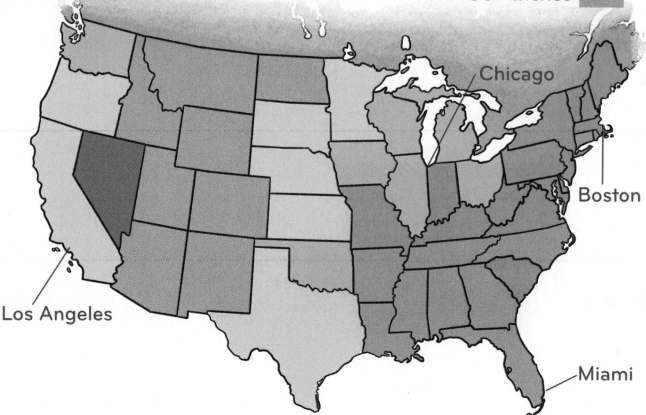

A bar graph is another way to compare precipitation in different places.

➤ **Use the bar graph below to answer the questions.**

Which city gets the most precipitation in April?

_____

How much rain does Boston get in July?

_____

What is the driest month in Miami?

_____

Which city gets the most precipitation in one year?

_____

When is the rainy season in Los Angeles?

_____

AVERAGE PRECIPITATION BY MONTH

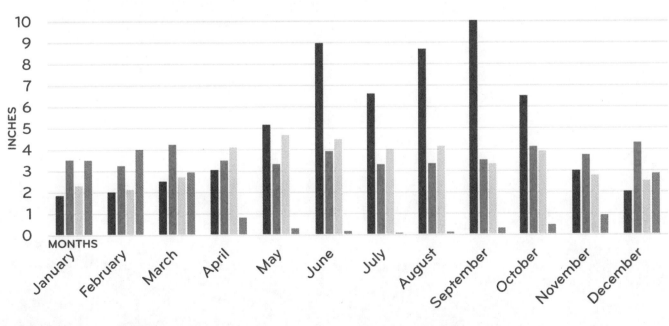

INCHES

10
9
8
7
6
5
4
3
2
1
0

MONTHS

January February March April May June July August September October November December

■ Miami   ■ Boston   ■ Chicago   ■ Los Angeles

Cloud Detective

Clouds are made up of water vapor. There are many different types of clouds, based on temperature, wind, amount of moisture, and air pressure. Clouds have different names depending on how high they form in the sky (the altitude) and what they look like from the ground.

Cirrus

Altostratus

Cumulonimbus

Cumulus

Stratus

➤ Use the cloud data sheet below to record the types of clouds you see on different days.

Date and Time

_____

_____

❏ None
❏ Altostratus
❏ Cirrus
❏ Cumulonimbus
❏ Cumulus
❏ Stratus

Date and Time

_____

_____

❏ None
❏ Altostratus
❏ Cirrus
❏ Cumulonimbus
❏ Cumulus
❏ Stratus

Date and Time

_____

_____

❏ None
❏ Altostratus
❏ Cirrus
❏ Cumulonimbus
❏ Cumulus
❏ Stratus

Date and Time

_____

_____

❏ None
❏ Altostratus
❏ Cirrus
❏ Cumulonimbus
❏ Cumulus
❏ Stratus

Date and Time

_____

_____

❏ None
❏ Altostratus
❏ Cirrus
❏ Cumulonimbus
❏ Cumulus
❏ Stratus

Date and Time

_____

_____

❏ None
❏ Altostratus
❏ Cirrus
❏ Cumulonimbus
❏ Cumulus
❏ Stratus

Measure the Wind

The Beaufort wind scale (ranging from 1 to 12) was created in 1805 to help sailors estimate wind speed based on what they could see. Here are things you might see as wind speed rises.

0 / CALM
0–1 mph*
Smoke rises straight up

1 / LIGHT AIR
1–3 mph
Smoke drifts; wind vanes don't move

2 / LIGHT BREEZE
4–7 mph
Wind felt on face; leaves rustle; wind vanes move

3 / GENTLE BREEZE
8–12 mph
Leaves and small twigs move; flags flap

4 / MODERATE BREEZE
13–18 mph
Dust and leaves fly around; small branches move

5 / FRESH BREEZE
19–24 mph
Small trees begin to sway

6 / STRONG BREEZE
25–31 mph
Big branches move; hard to hold an open umbrella

7 / NEAR GALE
32–38 mph
Whole trees in motion; hard to walk against the wind

8 / GALE
39–46 mph
Branches break off trees; hard to walk or move on foot

9 / SEVERE GALE
47–54 mph
Damage to buildings might occur

10 / STORM
55–63 mph
Trees uprooted; buildings damaged

11 / VIOLENT STORM
64–72 mph
Widespread damage

12 / HURRICANE
72 or more mph
Sustained winds as high as 150 mph

*mph = miles per hour

➤ Use the clues on page 36 to match the
pictures below with the wind speed. Fill
in the blanks with the correct number.

55–63
mph

Make a Wind Vane!

The direction of the wind is determined by where it is coming from, not where it is going. How do we figure out what direction the wind is coming from? We can notice a moving flag or leaves blowing in the air or look at a wind vane, which is an instrument that shows wind direction. Here's how to make your own wind vane.

HERE IS WHAT YOU WILL NEED.

Pencil, markers, scissors

Circle cut from a thick piece of cardboard or a heavy paper plate

2-foot-long streamer (ribbon, thick yarn, or strip of cloth)

Compass

Directions for making a wind vane.

1 Write the letter N for north at the top of the cardboard circle and the letter S for south at the bottom. Write W for west on the left and E for east on the right. These are the wind directions or cardinal points. If you want more detail, you can add additional directions between the cardinal points: NE, SE, SW, NW.

2 Decorate your wind vane if you wish. Poke a hole through the center of the circle with a pencil. Push the streamer through from the back of the circle. Tie it in a knot so the streamer hangs down.

3 To test your wind vane, go outdoors. Use a compass to find out where north is. Line up the N on your wind vane to face north. You'll see that south is behind you, west is on your left, and east is on your right.

4 Hold your plate over your head with the N facing north. Watch the streamer to see which way it moves. If the tail blows behind you to the south, you have a north wind.

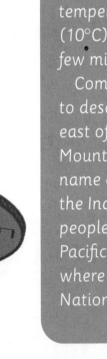

FUN FACT
A Chinook wind is a warm winter wind that can raise the temperature 50°F (10°C) in just a few minutes.
   Commonly used to describe winds east of the Rocky Mountains, the name comes from the Indigenous peoples of the Pacific Northwest, where the Chinook Nation lives.

Our Planet Earth

40

Weather Report

A meteorologist studies weather patterns and predicts changes. Now that you know more about the weather, you can practice being a meteorologist. Here are some questions to ask as you record data.

- What kinds of clouds do you see, if any?

- How windy is it?

- How else would you describe the weather today?

➤ Go outside and check the weather on different days. Answer the above questions as you fill out the weather notes for each day.

Date _____   Temperature _____

Circle
one:

Weather Notes

_____

_____

_____

Date

_____

Temperature

_____

Circle
one:

Weather Notes

_____

_____

_____

Date

_____

Temperature

_____

Circle
one:

Weather Notes

_____

_____

_____

Date

_____

Temperature

_____

Circle
one:

Weather Notes

_____

_____

BE A NATURE HERO

Take the Cool Earth, Cool Kids Challenge

See how many items on the checklist you can complete. The more you check off, the more you are helping the earth.

- ☐ Encourage your family to walk, bike, or take the bus or train instead of the car.

- ☐ Replace disposable products (like plastic sandwich bags) with reusable ones (washable containers or cloth bags).

- ☐ Reduce your energy consumption. Turn off lights and unplug electronics when not in use.

- ☐ Reduce waste by buying products in bigger packaging. Instead of individual yogurt tubs, buy a quart and put smaller servings into reusable containers.

- ☐ Have a trash pickup day around your neighborhood or schoolyard. Never pick up anything sharp!

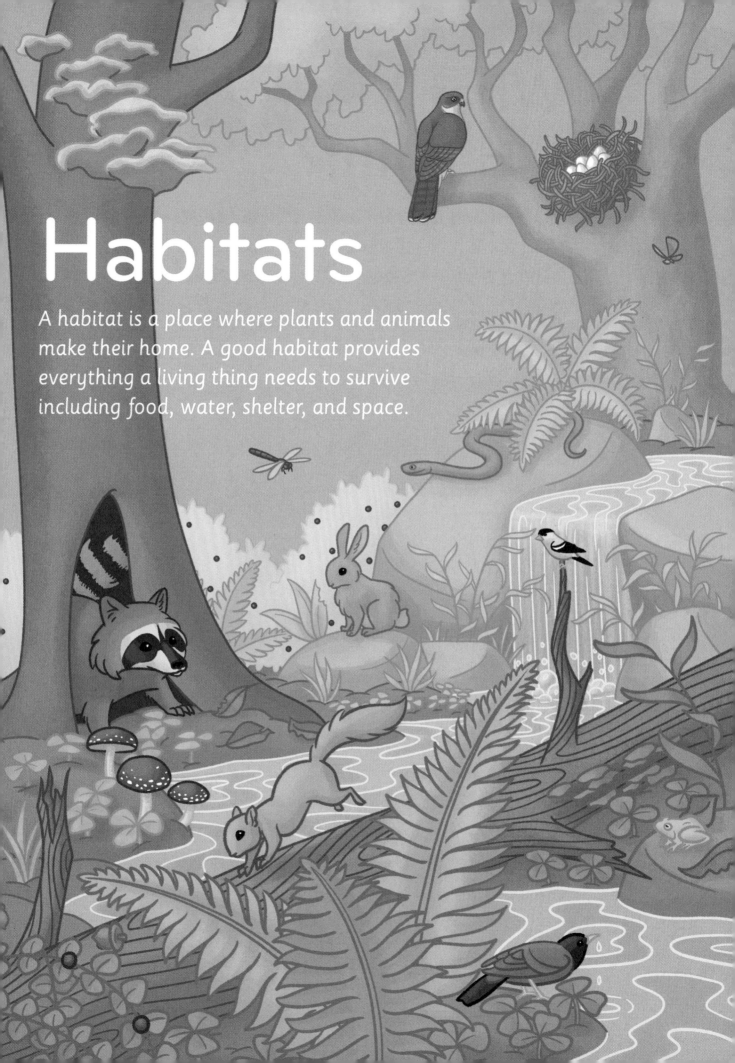

Habitats

A habitat is a place where plants and animals make their home. A good habitat provides everything a living thing needs to survive including food, water, shelter, and space.

What Makes a Habitat?

The world is filled with many different types of habitats. White-tailed deer and humans are both animals that need food, water, and shelter.

➤ Fill in the blanks with the word "deer" or "humans" to learn how deer and human habitats are different.

_____Deer_____ live in forests and near fields and other open spaces.

_____Humans_____ live in many different places, including rural areas, cities, and suburbs.

_____ eat leaves, grass, and bark.

_____ drink water from a pond or stream.

_____ grow food on farms or buy it in stores.

_____ usually get their water from plumbing/pipes in their homes.

_____ use tall grass and shrubs as shelter to help keep them safe.

_____ find safety and shelter in buildings with roofs and walls.

➤ How many deer are hidden in this habitat? Can you find a person, too?

DEER

Answer key on page 94

FUN FACT
The deer's coat is a reddish brown in the spring and summer. It turns grayish brown in the fall and winter. This helps them camouflage in different seasons.

46

Answer
key on
page 94

Habitat Mix-Up

Every living thing has particular needs for its habitat. Plants need appropriate temperatures, soil quality, and rainfall to thrive. Animals have to be able to find food and places to live.

➤ Draw an X through the plants and animals that don't belong in the habitats shown here.

FRESHWATER POND HABITAT

Answer
key on
page 94

FUN FACT
Some animals
migrate from one
habitat to another
when the seasons
change.

DESERT HABITAT

GARDEN HABITAT

48

Answer
key on
page 94

Who Eats What in a Food Web?

Plants and animals all need energy to grow and move around. An important part of any habitat is a food web, which shows how energy flows from one source to another. For example, a small bird gets energy from eating berries and seeds. A larger bird gets energy from eating the smaller bird.

Here are some examples of how a food web works in a pond.

- Water plants provide food for ducks, grasshoppers, snails, and muskrats.

- Snapping turtles eat fish, frogs, snakes, and ducks.

- Frogs and some fish eat snails and water bugs.

- Herons and kingfishers eat fish, frogs, and dragonflies.

➤ **Draw lines with arrows to show who eats what in this pond habitat.**

Neighborhood Nature Scavenger Hunt

It's fun to explore your neighborhood and to look for clues about wildlife that lives near you. You might find nuts or seeds, feathers, nests in trees and shrubs, holes in the ground, or even animal poop.

Make a game of your search by playing Nature Bingo. Play alone or make copies of the Bingo card page and invite some friends to join you for a nature adventure in your neighborhood!

FUN FACT
The scientific term for animal droppings, or poop, is **SCAT**. Different animals leave behind different types of scat.

➤ Look around your neighborhood for signs of wildlife, like tracks, feathers, sources of food and water, or a place where an animal might live. When you see one, mark an X across the matching Bingo square. Three in a row wins!

NATURE BINGO

 ANIMAL TRACK	 FEATHER	SOURCE OF WATER
 SOURCE OF FOOD	FREE SPACE	 NEST
 HOLE IN THE GROUND	 ANIMAL SOUND	 SCAT

BE A NATURE HERO

Help Make a Habitat

Even though many animals have an amazing ability to adapt to changes in their habitats, issues such as habitat destruction and climate change can make it difficult for animals to find what they need. By providing resources that are in short supply or helping animals get the resources they cannot find elsewhere, you are being a nature hero!

Think about some of the animals that you observed on your Neighborhood Nature Scavenger Hunt (page 50). What do they eat? Where do they get their water? What do they use for shelter? What can you do to improve their habitat? Here are some suggestions.

★ Put up a nest box.

★ Make a bird feeder.

★ Set up a water station.

★ Make a brush pile for small mammals and insects.

★ Plant wildflowers for pollinators.

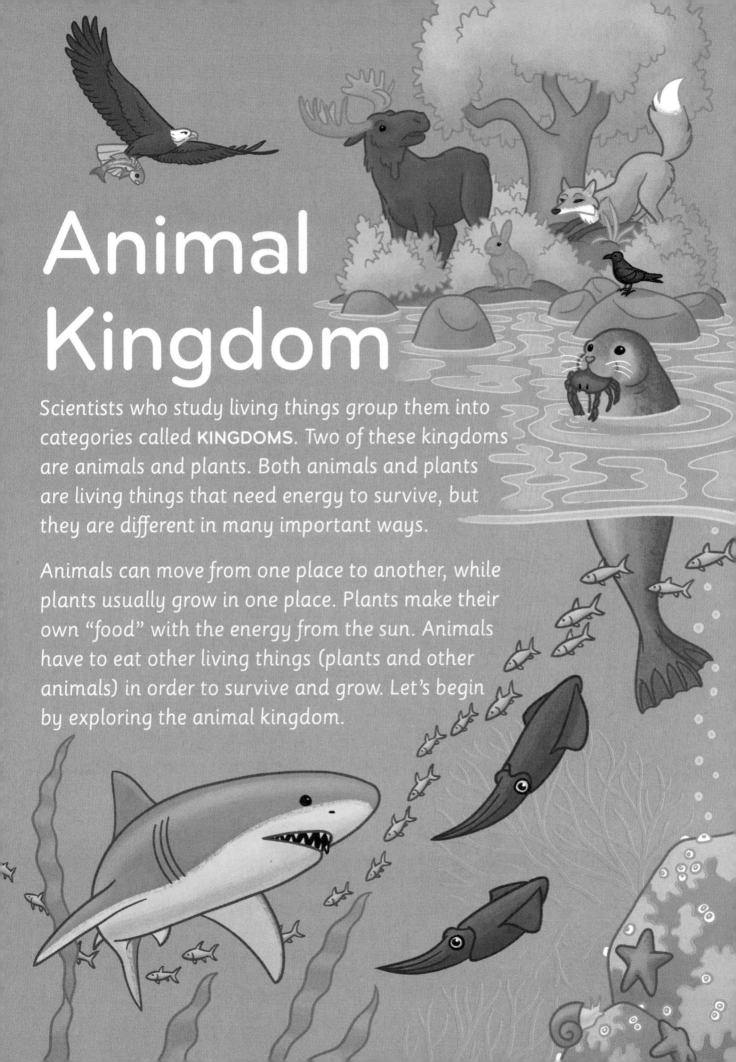

Animal Kingdom

Scientists who study living things group them into categories called **KINGDOMS**. Two of these kingdoms are animals and plants. Both animals and plants are living things that need energy to survive, but they are different in many important ways.

Animals can move from one place to another, while plants usually grow in one place. Plants make their own "food" with the energy from the sun. Animals have to eat other living things (plants and other animals) in order to survive and grow. Let's begin by exploring the animal kingdom.

Vertebrate or Invertebrate?

Animals that have backbones, such as mammals, fish, and reptiles, are called **VERTEBRATES**. They have bones inside their bodies, called a **SKELETON**, that protect their organs and support their bodies.

Animals that do not have a backbone are called **INVERTEBRATES**. Some invertebrates, like crabs, grasshoppers, and millipedes, have an **EXOSKELETON** on the outside of their bodies for protection and support. Others, like slugs and jellyfish, have soft, squishy bodies because they don't have exoskeletons.

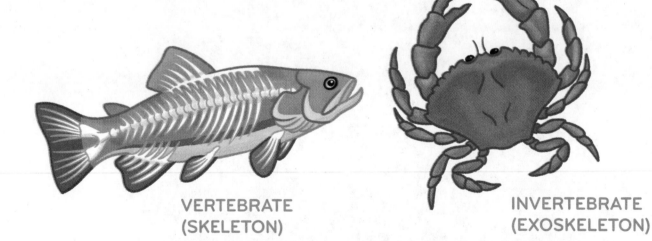

VERTEBRATE
(SKELETON)

INVERTEBRATE
(EXOSKELETON)

FUN FACT

Don't be fooled! Animals like armadillos and turtles are vertebrates with backbones. Their shells are adaptations for protection that are made of bone and attached to their backbones.

➤ Draw a square around the vertebrates.
Draw a circle around the invertebrates.

➤ How many vertebrates are there?

➤ How many invertebrates are there?

What Kind of Vertebrate Is This?

There are five main classes or groups of vertebrates. The classes are mammal, bird, reptile, amphibian, and fish. Each class has distinct characteristics. Here are a few ways to tell which animals belong to which class.

MAMMALS have fur or hair. They are born live (not hatched from an egg). Mammals make milk for their babies.

BIRDS have feathers. They lay eggs that have hard shells.

REPTILES have scaly skin. They lay eggs with rubbery shells. They breathe air through lungs.

AMPHIBIANS have smooth or slightly bumpy skin. Most lay their jellylike eggs in water and spend the beginning of their life cycle there. Most adult amphibians breathe through lungs and live partly on land.

FISH have scales on the outside of their bodies. They live and lay their eggs in water and breathe through gills. They have fins for swimming.

➤ Using the clues on page 56, fill in the class for each animal.

Fish

Animal Kingdom

58

Can You Camouflage?

Camouflage is a way that animals protect themselves from predators, or disguise themselves when hunting prey. Being camouflaged means that other animals can't see you because you blend in with your background.

➤ Color in each white blob so that it is camouflaged.

FUN FACT
A crab spider can slowly change its color to match the flower it is hunting on.

Animal Kingdom

60

Tracks Tell a Tale

Four-legged mammals typically leave one of four track patterns. Knowing the patterns can help you guess which mammal has been through an area even if you can't identify the specific track.

WALKERS like coyotes and bobcats move their opposite feet diagonally, with left and right paws on opposite sides of an invisible line. The front and back tracks often overlap.

HOPPERS like rabbits, mice, and squirrels make a pattern with two small front feet behind the two larger back feet.

BOUNDERS are in the weasel family and usually have two feet together (front feet, back feet).

WADDLERS include animals like bears, raccoons, and skunks. They move the front and back feet on one side and then the front and back feet on the other, creating parallel tracks.

➤ The tracks left by animals can tell a story of where they've been and what they've done. Follow the tracks to find out which animal made them.

Make a Track Station

Do you know what animals live near your home? Many animals come out at night to look for food. By setting up a track station, you may be able to find out who visits when you're not around to see them. Try setting up several different track stations using different bait.

HERE IS WHAT YOU WILL NEED.

Ruler

Bait to attract animals
(cut-up fruit and vegetables, peanuts, birdseed, oatmeal)

5-pound bag of flour

Fine-mesh colander

Directions for making a track station.

1 Find a spot near a tree or a pile of rocks. Use the colander to sprinkle the whole bag of flour evenly over an area about 3 feet by 3 feet. Spread it thickly enough to cover the ground.

2 Put some bait in the middle of the flour.

3 Come back the next day to see if any animals walked through the flour and left tracks.

➤ Use the chart below to record any tracks you see. Look for patterns in the way the animal walked across the flour.

Date _____   Size of track _____

What type of track pattern? _____

....

Date _____   Size of track _____

What type of track pattern? _____

....

Date _____   Size of track _____

What type of track pattern? _____

Try to Fly!

Many animals have wings to fly with, but the sizes and shapes of wings vary greatly. Different types of wings mean different ways of flying. Some animals flap their wings, others flutter them.

RUBY-THROATED HUMMINGBIRDS move their wings very fast. They can hover in place while they drink nectar out of flowers, and they can fly backward!

➤ Pretend to fly like a ruby-throated hummingbird! Flap your arms as fast as you can while hovering in place. Keep flapping while you move forward and backward.

LITTLE BROWN BATS do something unusual when flying. The upstroke (when the wing moves up) is faster than the downstroke (when the wing moves down).

➤ Pretend to fly like a little brown bat by moving your arms up quickly and down a little more slowly.

MONARCH BUTTERFLIES have large wings for their body size. When they flap, their wings move all the way up and all the way down. They don't fly in a straight line, but move up and down through the air.

➤ Try moving your arms all the way up and down like a monarch butterfly. Now "fly" in a zigzag pattern.

Wing Math

The measurement from wingtip to wingtip is called the **WINGSPAN**. Some birds have very long wings. Once they are in the sky, these birds can soar through the air for a long time without flapping their wings at all!

➤ Answer the questions about these different soaring birds.

BROWN PELICAN
7 feet

CALIFORNIA
CONDOR
10 feet

TURKEY
VULTURE
6 feet

Which bird has the widest wingspan?

_____

How much wider is the California condor's wingspan than the brown pelican's wingspan?

_____

How wide is the wingspan of two turkey vultures added together?

_____

➤ Calculate the solution to each word problem.

Ruby-throated hummingbirds can flap their wings about 60 times in 1 second. How many times can a hummingbird flap its wings in 10 seconds?

60 × 10 = ☐

Little brown bats can flap their wings 12 times per second. How many wing flaps does a little brown bat make in 8 seconds? How about in 1 minute? (Think: There are 60 seconds in a minute.)

12 × 8 = ☐

12 × 60 = ☐

FUN FACTS
Owls have very soft feathers, so their flight is silent.
    Falcons tuck their wings to swoop down on prey at blazing speeds.

When a monarch butterfly is moving fast, it flaps its wings up to 12 times per second. When migrating over long distances, it flies slower to save energy, only flapping 4 times per second. How many times would it flap its wings over 1 minute when it is migrating?

60 × 4 = ☐

Fabulous Feathers

Feathers come in many shapes and sizes, from strong wing feathers to fluffy down. The form and structure of each feather is related to its function (what it is meant to do).

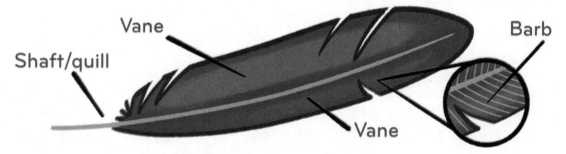

Vane

Shaft/quill

Barb

Vane

PRIMARY WING FEATHERS are smooth and strong. One vane is very narrow and the other is wider. This structure aids in flying.

TAIL FEATHERS have vanes that are similar in width. The ends can be round, square, or pointed. Birds use their tails to brake and steer.

CONTOUR FEATHERS cover the bird's body. Contour feathers give shape and provide a smooth surface.

DOWN FEATHERS grow next to the skin. They are extra soft and fluffy for warmth.

➤ Using the clues on page 68, fill in the blanks to identify each type of feather.

Using the clues on page 68

FUN FACT
When a bird is cold, it fluffs up its feathers to trap warm air next to its skin.

Animal Kingdom

69

Answer key on page 95

Answer key on page 95

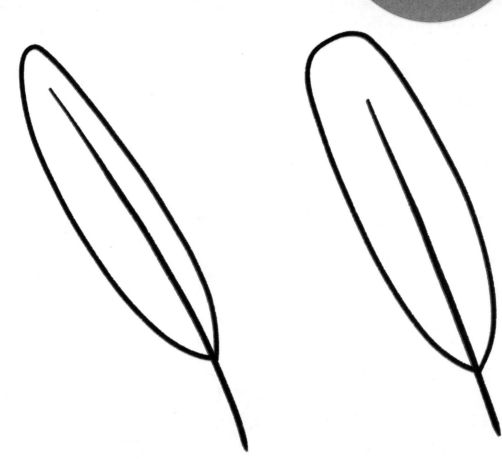

_____

_____

Flap a Feather

Try making feathers out of different kinds of paper. See how many different feathers you can make and then experiment with how different shapes and materials react in the wind and air.

HERE IS WHAT YOU WILL NEED.

Several types of paper of varying thickness (tissue paper, notepaper, construction paper, light cardboard)

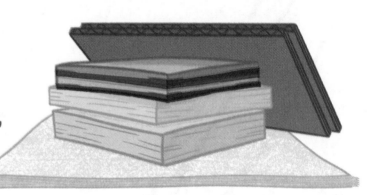

Colored pencils or markers for decorating

Scissors and glue

Toothpicks, wooden skewers, or pipe cleaners

Directions for making feathers.

1 Draw a feather shape on a piece of light cardboard and cut it out. Trace the shape onto two or three other types of paper and cut those feathers out. Make more feathers using a different shape. (See page 68.)

2 Cut slits around the edges of some of your feathers to see how it affects a feather's movement. Leave some feathers with smooth edges.

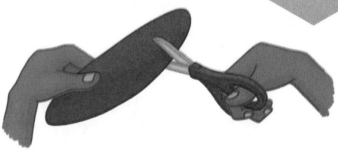

3 If you want one or more of your feathers to have a rigid shaft, glue a toothpick or a piece of wooden skewer or pipe cleaner in the center.

4 Now it's time to experiment. Drop each feather from a few feet off the floor. Now take your feathers outside and see what happens when you drop them.

• How do the different shapes act when they fall?

• What happens if the air is moving?

Bird Beaks

Bird beaks can tell you a lot about what types of foods an animal might eat. The shapes and function of a beak are as diverse as tools in the kitchen or a tool belt!

Here are a few different types of birds and their beaks.

HUMMINGBIRDS have long, thin beaks to reach into flowers and drink liquid nectar.

GOLDFINCHES have short, strong, cone-shaped beaks for cracking open seeds.

GREAT BLUE HERONS have long, strong, pointed beaks for precision strikes on fish or frogs in the water.

DUCKS have wide beaks with comblike edges. When a duck scoops up water and closes its beak, the water drains out and bugs and plants are trapped.

HAWKS have sharp, hooked beaks for cutting and tearing their prey.

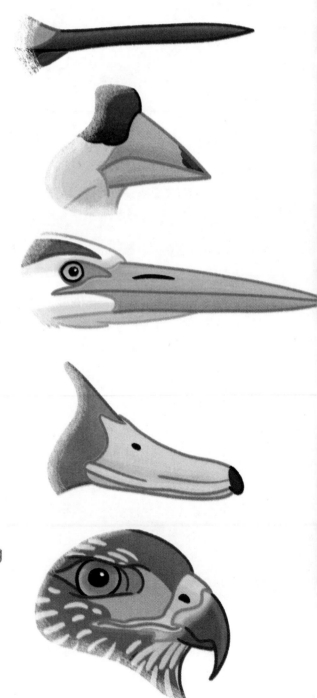

➤ Using the clues on page 72, draw a line from the beak shape to the tool that matches it.

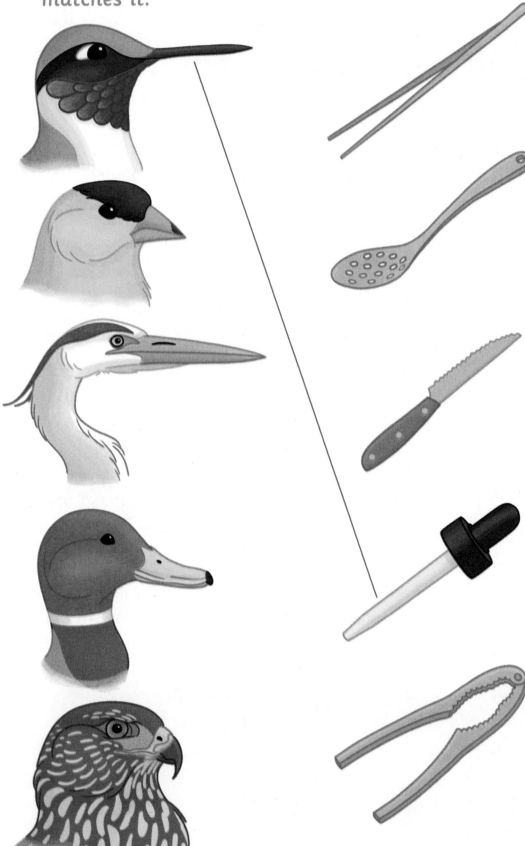

BE A NATURE HERO

Write to Your Legislator

Elected officials rely on all citizens to tell them what issues are important. You can write a letter to your elected representatives to tell them what you care about in your community. Here's an example.

Dear [Name of Legislator],

People used to like to look at the river in our town and enjoyed swimming in it. We cannot do that anymore because people throw litter and dump chemicals and other pollution into the river. It is not good for the animals around it and it is ruining our community. The whole food chain is affected.

I think we should pass a law where people would be called to volunteer to clean up the river, just like they have to do jury duty. Also, there should be a hotline people can call when they see people polluting and littering. Then people who are caught polluting would have to clean it up and pay a fee.

Thank you for taking the time to read my letter. I hope you will talk to the other representatives about this problem. We need a healthy river!

Sincerely,
[Your Name]

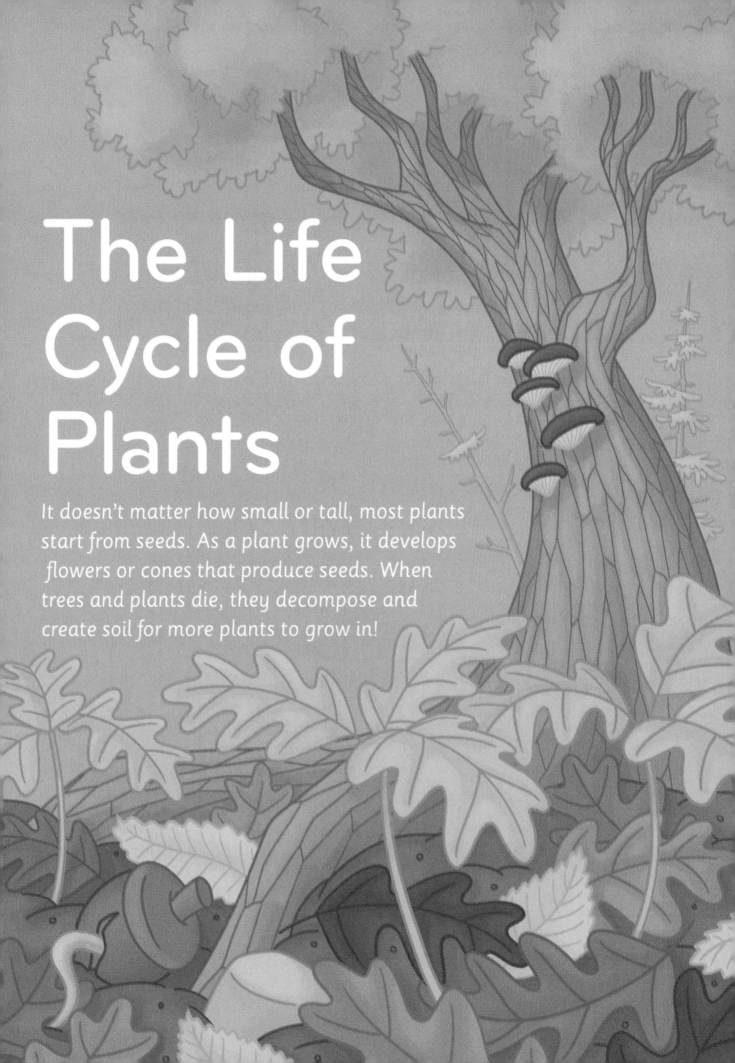

The Life Cycle of Plants

It doesn't matter how small or tall, most plants start from seeds. As a plant grows, it develops flowers or cones that produce seeds. When trees and plants die, they decompose and create soil for more plants to grow in!

From Seeds to Plants

Most plants come from seeds. Seeds have an outer covering that protects a tiny plant inside. With water and warmth, the tiny plant **GERMINATES** (starts to grow). Roots push downward into the soil. The stem grows upward and develops leaves.

➤ Starting with the flowers, number the pictures in order to show how a flowering tree grows.

FLOWERING TREE CYCLE

Sapling grows.

Seed falls to the ground.

Tree grows flowers. 1

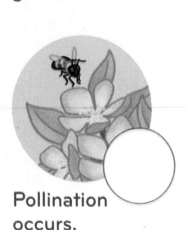

Pollination occurs.

Fruit forms around seed.

The Life
Cycle of
Plants

77

Answer
key on
page 95

When the plant is fully grown, it makes more seeds from flowers or cones. The flowers or cones are **POLLINATED** by animals, insects, or the wind. The seeds develop and drop to the ground, where they can grow into a new plant and start the cycle over again.

➤ Starting with the cones, number the pictures in order to show how a cone-bearing tree grows.

CONE-BEARING TREE CYCLE

Pollination occurs.

Tree grows cones.

1

Sapling grows.

Seeds spread by wind or animals.

Seeds develop.

Let's Look at Grass

We may not think of grasses as being flowering plants, but they are! They don't have showy flowers like a fruit tree, but they do produce seeds. Grasses are pollinated by wind.

Grasses grow in almost every part of the world. They provide food for many animals, including humans. Rice, wheat, corn, and oats are all grasses. Grass plants have many of the same parts as other plants.

STEM: carries water and nutrients to and from the roots and the leaves

ROOTS: draw water and nutrients from the soil and hold the plant in place

RHIZOME: a sideways underground stem that grows roots and produces new grass plants

STOLON: a sideways stem above the ground that grows roots and produces new grass plants

FLOWER: where seeds are produced

BLADE: a leaf of the plant that makes food

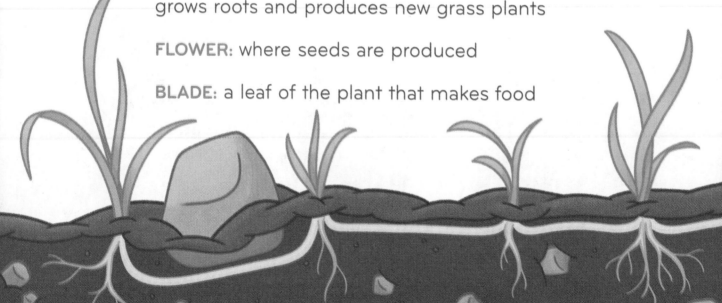

➤ Use the descriptions on page 78 to identify the parts of a grass plant. Write the names of the correct parts in the blanks below.

FUN FACTS
There are over 9,000 known species of grass.
 Bamboo is a grass that can grow to be 100 feet tall!
 Sugarcane is a type of grass that is used to make sugar.

Seed and Plant Math

Practice your math skills with trees, seeds, and plants. Go outside to create math problems on your own using natural objects!

➤ Find the sum or difference to solve each word problem.

Before the windstorm, the maple tree had 50 leaves on its branches. After the windstorm, the maple tree had 21 leaves on its branches. How many leaves blew off of the tree's branches?

$$50 - 21 = \boxed{}$$

There are 20 apples on the apple tree. Each apple has 5 seeds. How many seeds did the tree produce in all?

$$20 \times 5 = \boxed{}$$

For a morning meal, a cardinal ate 12 seeds from a sunflower, 8 seeds from a coneflower, and 5 seeds from a stalk of grass. How many seeds did the cardinal eat?

$$12 + 8 + 5 = \boxed{}$$

A milkweed pod has 225 seeds. If 113 seeds fly away with the wind, how many seeds are left behind?

$$225 - 113 = \boxed{}$$

In a small park, there are 22 oak trees, 5 maple trees, and 30 pine trees. How many trees are in the park?

$$22 + 5 + 30 = \boxed{}$$

Know Your Plant Parts

Plants are made up of several different parts.
Each part has a job.

FLOWER: makes seeds for the plant

FRUIT: attracts animals so seeds are spread

LEAF: makes food for the plant with sunlight, water, and carbon dioxide from the air

STEM: supports the plant and carries food and water

SEED: the part of the plant that could grow into another plant

ROOT: stabilizes the plant, soaks up water and minerals, and stores food

What Plant Part Are You Eating?

What part of the plant do these different foods come from?

➤ Draw a line from each food to the correct plant part.

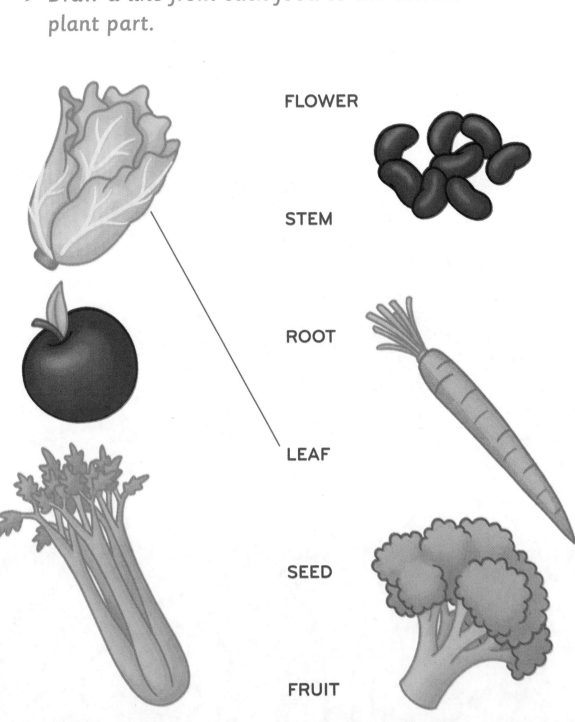

FLOWER

STEM

ROOT

LEAF

SEED

FRUIT

Tree Cookie Detective

Each spring and summer, a tree adds new layers of wood to its trunk. By looking at a "slice" of tree, sometimes called a "tree cookie," you can learn a lot about a tree's life.

In the spring, growth is fast, the plant cells are larger, and the rings are lighter in color. Later in the summer, growth is slower, and the rings are darker.

Spring growth ring

Summer growth ring

The Life
Cycle of
Plants

85

Answer
key on
page 96

The rings are very close together when the tree grows more slowly. Sometimes that's because there was a drought, so the tree didn't get enough water.

➤ Draw a circle around an area on the tree slice where there might have been a drought.

If you count the dark rings from the center to the outside, you can estimate how old the tree is!

➤ How old was this tree when it was cut down?

YEARS

The Life
Cycle of
Plants

86

Answer
key on
page 96

Beetle Mania

Some kinds of beetles burrow into trees to lay their eggs, leaving winding tracks through the wood. Woodpeckers peck into the tree to eat insects.

➤ Help the woodpecker get to the beetle.

A Hidden Habitat

A fallen log on the forest floor might look like just a dead piece of wood. But if you look closer, you will discover a hidden habitat. Fallen logs and branches slowly **DECOMPOSE** (break down and turn into soil). During that process, they provide food and shelter for plants and animals of all sizes.

➤ One log can support many different organisms. Draw a line from the word to the drawing of each plant or animal.

MOSS

LICHEN

PINE SEEDLINGS

MUSHROOMS

BEETLE

CENTIPEDE

ANTS

SALAMANDER

SLUG

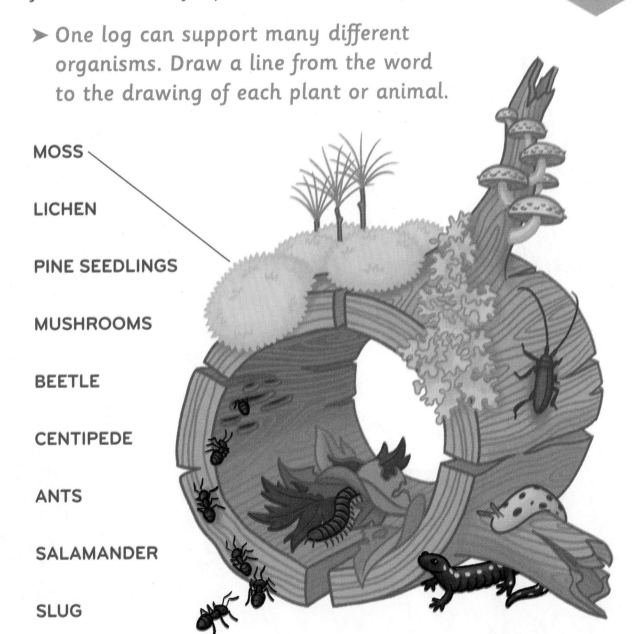

The Power of Plants

Plants and trees are important to our lives. They provide oxygen so we can breathe, and they create habitat for wildlife. They also give us many products that we use every day. For example, every time you open a book (including this one!), you can thank a tree.

➤ Match each product with the plant or tree it came from.

Thank a Plant

What is your favorite thing that comes from a plant? Is it chocolate, or your favorite T-shirt, or the best book you ever read? What plant does your favorite thing come from?

➤ Write a thank-you letter or draw a picture to tell that plant how much you appreciate it!

Leaf Pressing

One of the best parts of fall is the amazing leaf colors. Sadly, just as quickly as the leaves turn red, yellow, and orange, they drop to the ground and turn brown. How can you make the fall colors last just a little longer?

➤ Try pressing some of your favorite leaves and making a collage!

HERE IS WHAT YOU WILL NEED.

Small bag for collecting plants

Paper towels or parchment paper

Heavy books or binders for stacking

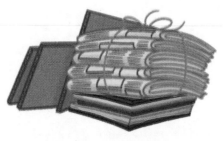

Recycled newspaper, construction paper, or cardboard

Glue

Directions for pressing leaves.

1 Collect fallen leaves, plants, or flowers. Look for various colors and shapes, and items that will press flat easily.

2 Lay your plant collection out flat between sheets of paper towel or parchment paper, making sure the plants don't overlap. Stack some heavy books or binders on top to help remove excess moisture and keep your items flat. Leave them like this for at least 6 hours.

3 Gently remove the items from between the paper towels. Arrange the plants on a piece of paper or cardboard to make a collage picture.

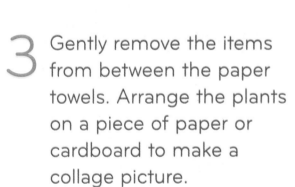

4 Carefully lift up each plant piece and add a thin layer of glue to the back. Stick each piece to the paper. Let the collage dry for about 1 hour before hanging it up to enjoy it.

BE A NATURE HERO

Be a Community Scientist

Scientists need to gather a lot of data when they study nature, and sometimes they need the help of lots of people. So if you like nature and want to learn more, you can help scientists who study nature.

Community science research projects rely on data collected by people that are shared directly with scientists. Anyone can be a community scientist—all it takes is good observation skills and the ability to record your observations with paper and pen or a device like a phone or tablet.

Check out SciStarter, a community science database where you can find research projects on a variety of topics, from recording bloom times to watching wildlife to observing the night sky. You can even find projects that are taking place near you! Here's the link: https://scistarter.org/.

Answer Key

PAGES 6–7

PAGE 15

PAGES 8–9

PAGE 19

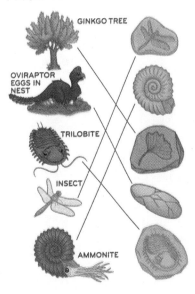

PAGES 10–11

SANDSTONE

QUARTZITE

OBSIDIAN

GNEISS   GRANITE   CONGLOMERATE

PAGES 12–13

Where's the metamorphic rock? It melted into a pool of magma.

▼ Start here.
Hot magma in the earth erupts from a volcano as lava.

Deep in the earth under extreme heat and pressure, sedimentary rock turns into METAMORPHIC rock.

The lava cools and hardens into IGNEOUS rock.

Over a long time, layers of sediment build up and get squished under lots of other layers. Now it is a SEDIMENTARY rock.

For a long time, the igneous rock is weathered by wind and water.

The pieces get smaller and smaller. Finally, the river deposits them as SEDIMENT.

Rock pieces are eroded away and carried into a fast-moving river.

PAGE 27

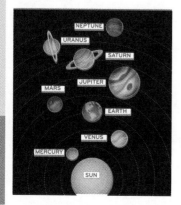

PAGE 29

PAGE 31

Evaporation
Condensation
Precipitation
Bodies of Water

PAGE 32

Nevada

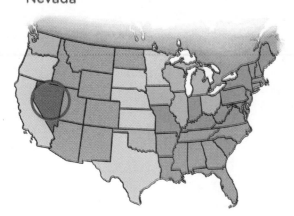

PAGE 33

Chicago
3.5 inches
January
Miami
Winter

PAGE 37

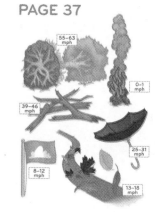

PAGES 44–45

Deer
Deer
Humans
Humans
Deer
Humans

8
DEER

PAGES 46–47

PAGES 48–49

PAGE 55

6 vertebrates
6 invertebrates

PAGE 57

BIRD · BIRD · REPTILE
REPTILE · AMPHIBIAN · AMPHIBIAN
MAMMAL · MAMMAL · FISH

PAGE 61

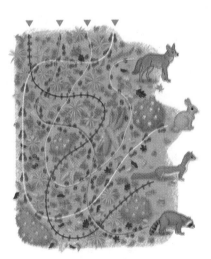

PAGES 66–67

California condor	60 × 10 = 600
3 feet	12 × 8 = 96
12 feet	12 × 60 = 720
	60 × 4 = 240

PAGE 69

PRIMARY WING FEATHER · TAIL FEATHER
DOWN FEATHER · CONTOUR FEATHER

PAGE 73

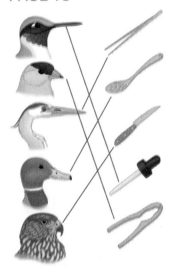

PAGES 76–77

5 · 4

2 · 3 · 1

2 · 1

4 · 3 · 5

PAGE 79

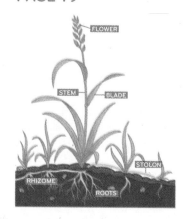

PAGES 80–81

50 – 21 = 29

20 × 5 = 100

12 + 8 + 5 = 25

225 – 113 = 112

22 + 5 + 30 = 57

PAGE 83

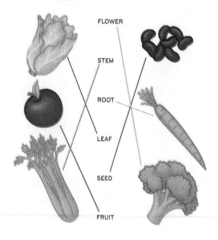

PAGES 84–85

PAGE 86

PAGE 87

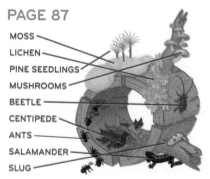

PAGE 88